religion in focus
christianity

Geoff Teece

A⁺

First published in 2003 by Franklin Watts
Franklin Watts, 96 Leonard Street, London EC2A 4XD

Franklin Watts Australia
45–51 Huntley Street, Alexandria, NSW 2015
This edition published under license from Franklin Watts. All rights reserved.

Series Editor: Adrian Cole; Designer: Proof Books; Art Director: Jonathan Hair; Consultants: Alan Brown, University College, Worcester and Friar Martin Ganeri, O.P.; Picture Researcher: Diana Morris

Published in the United States by Smart Apple Media
1980 Lookout Drive, North Mankato, Minnesota 56003

Library of Congress Cataloging-in-Publication Data

Teece, Geoff.
Christianity / by Geoff Teece.
p. cm. — (Religion in focus)
Includes index.
Contents: Jesus of Nazareth—Christian beliefs—Christian values and character—The disciples—The Bible—The Church—Different forms of worship—Worship: the Eucharist—Christian festivals (November–March/April)—Christian festivals (March/April–October)—Sacred places—Life rituals—Christian denominations.
ISBN 1-58340-465-1
1. Christianity—Juvenile literature. [1. Christianity.] I. Series.

BR125.5.T44 2004
230—dc22   2003190052

9 8 7 6 5 4 3 2 1

Acknowledgments
The publishers would like to thank the following for permission to reproduce photographs in this book:

Bibliothèque Nationale, Paris/Bridgeman Art Library: 12.
British Library/Bridgeman Art Library: 24.
Chris Fairclough: 19b.
Gudbjartur Gunnarsson/Trip: 13.
Haga/A1pix: 11, 21.
Hanan Isachar/Corbis: 5.
Carlos Reyes-Manzo/Andes Press Agency: 8, 9, 16t, 16b, 17, 25, 27.
Museo de Arte de Catalunya, Barcelona/Bridgeman Art Library: 3, 10.
Mark Peterson/Corbis SABA: 23.
H. Rogers/Trip: 20, 26.
Santa Maria della Grazie, Milan/Bridgeman Art Library: 22.
Steve Shott Photography: front and back cover, 1, 2, 6, 7, 18, 19.
Sipa/Rex Features: 15.

Contents

Jesus of Nazareth

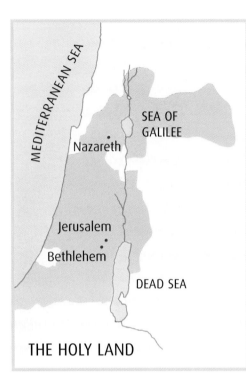

THE HOLY LAND

Christians believe that Jesus of Nazareth was the Son of God, and remembering and celebrating his life is essential to Christian worship. Jesus lived over 2,000 years ago in Judea, where Israel and Palestine are today, from about 4 B.C. to A.D. 30.

THE BIRTH OF JESUS

Jesus was born in Bethlehem (*see left*). His parents, Mary and Joseph, had traveled to Bethlehem from Nazareth to be counted for a census. An angel told a group of shepherds that the Son of God had been born nearby, and they hurried to see the baby. Further away, some wise men saw a star in the east and followed it to worship Jesus. Herod, the king of Judea, felt threatened and ordered his soldiers to kill all baby boys in that area—an event referred to as the "Massacre of the Innocents." However, Joseph dreamt about it and escaped to Egypt with Mary and Jesus. After Herod's death they returned to Nazareth, where Joseph continued his trade as a carpenter.

THE VIRGIN MARY

Jesus's mother is known as the "Virgin Mary." St. Luke's Gospel records that the Angel Gabriel (the messenger of good news) announced to Mary that she would have a child who would be the Son of God, even though she was a virgin. Mary has a special place in some Christian traditions because she is the mother of Jesus. Some Christians pray to God through Mary.

THE VIRGIN MARY
Mary has a special place in the hearts of many Christians.

TEACHING

When he was about 30 years old, Jesus left Nazareth. His cousin John baptized him in the river Jordan. Then Jesus went into the desert to think. For 40 days he went without food, and the devil tempted him three times. But Jesus rejected the devil, saying, "Get behind me, Satan."

When Jesus returned home, he chose 12 followers, or disciples (*see pages 10–11*), to travel with him, teaching a simple message based on loving God and your neighbor. He healed the sick and even raised people from the dead. These extraordinary events are called miracles.

THE LAST SUPPER

The last meal Jesus had with his disciples is now called the Last Supper. During the meal Jesus told his disciples that he was going to be killed. He shared bread and wine with them and told them to do this after his death in memory of him. Christians still do this regularly. It is called Mass, Holy Communion, or the Eucharist (*see pages 18–19*).

CRUCIFIXION AND RESURRECTION

The next day, Jesus was arrested after being betrayed by Judas, one of his disciples. Jesus was found guilty of breaking religious laws and challenging Roman authority. He was crucified; nailed to a cross and left to die.

Jesus's body was taken to a tomb, but three days later his disciples returned to find it empty. They believed he had come back to life. The Gospels record appearances after his death. His return is known as the Resurrection and is celebrated today, especially at Easter (*pages 20–23*).

TWO REASONS FOR JESUS'S ARREST

1. The Jews' relationship with God was based on strict religious laws. Jesus taught that a good relationship with God was based on love, not these restrictive laws.

2. The Romans were occupying the kingdom of Israel, but allowed the Jews to practice their religion as long as they did not threaten Roman rule. The Romans disliked religious leaders such as Jesus because they upset the stability of Israel.

GETHSEMANE
The garden where Jesus was betrayed and arrested.

THE GOSPELS

The story of Jesus's life and teachings is contained in the four Gospels. These form part of the Bible, the Christians' holy book (*see pages 12–13*). The word "gospel" means "good news." The Gospels were written by four of Jesus's disciples to spread the good news about Jesus.

THE FOUR GOSPELS	WRITTEN AROUND
Mark	A.D. 65–75
Matthew	A.D. 85
Luke	A.D. 80–90
John	A.D. 100

Christian beliefs

PRAYING TO JESUS
Some Christians offer their prayers to God with the words, "In the name of Our Lord Jesus Christ, amen."

Christians believe that there is only one God, who is the Creator of everything. The world depends on God, all life comes from God, and human beings have a special place in his world, with a responsibility to look after it.

GOD AS THE HOLY TRINITY

Christians often call God "Father." This is because he is the father of Jesus—and of all Christians. The Nicene Creed, a statement of belief written by early Christians, refers to God the Father, God the Son, and God the Holy Spirit. This is called the Holy Trinity. The first Christians did not want to say that there was more than one God, but they did want to make it clear that God, Jesus, and the Holy Spirit were different aspects of God.

THE NICENE CREED (excerpt)

We believe in one Lord, Jesus Christ,
the only Son of God,
eternally begotten of the Father,
God from God, Light from Light,
true God from true God,
begotten not made,
of one Being with the Father.

THE HOLY SPIRIT

Christians have different ideas about the Holy Spirit. In the creeds the Holy Spirit is the third part of the Trinity and is referred to as "the giver of life." Christians believe that Jesus was full of the Holy Spirit and is active in the world today through the power of the Holy Spirit.

WHAT IS GOD LIKE?

Christians' closest understanding of God is found in Jesus, whom they believe was God. Jesus's example and actions inspire and motivate Christians to live a good Christian life. Many Christians believe that Jesus is their friend, supporter, and guide through everything they do in life. Belief in Jesus as a living, resurrected person lies at the heart of their faith.

JESUS AS GOD INCARNATE

Christians believe that Jesus was God incarnate—he was God made flesh. Other titles given to Jesus include Lord, Savior, Messiah, and Christ. "Christ" is taken from a Greek word meaning "Anointed One" or "Chosen One."

HUMANS AND SIN

In the Bible, the story of Adam and Eve tells how humans became separated from God. God made Adam and Eve, and at first they were obedient to him. But then they were tempted by a serpent and disobeyed God's orders. So God cast them out of their home, an earthly paradise called Eden. Ever since, humans have tried to regain this original state of bliss. People have a habit of turning away from God, just as Adam and Eve did, and pleasing themselves. This is called "sin" and it leads to wrongdoing. God sent his son, Jesus, to lead people away from sin and to re-establish the link between humans and God. Jesus did this through his life, death, and resurrection. He taught people to think of God and others before themselves.

JESUS IS FOR EVERYBODY

Christians believe that Jesus is for all people at all times and in all places. The Gospels record Jesus's dealings with non-Jews (gentiles) and outcasts of all kinds, even though he knew he would be criticized for treating such people with love and kindness. His actions illustrate the Christian belief that all people are the children of God.

STATUE OF JESUS
Many churches have a statue of Jesus.

THE CROSS

Different Christian traditions highlight various aspects of Jesus's life, but they are all united by the powerful symbol of the cross. In Roman Catholic churches a crucifix (*left*, a cross with the figure of Jesus on it) reminds worshipers that Jesus suffered and died for them. In Anglican churches a plain cross (*right*) reminds the congregation that Jesus overcame death and evil by rising from the dead.

Christian values and character

When someone asked Jesus what is the greatest commandment he replied, "Love the Lord your God with all your heart, with all your soul, and with all your mind. This is the greatest and most important commandment. The second most important commandment is like it: Love your neighbor as you love yourself." (Matthew 22: 37–39)

Living a life devoted to God is about having particular values and developing a certain type of character. St. Paul (*see page 11*) wrote: "The Spirit produces love, joy, peace, patience, kindness, goodness, faithfulness, humility, and self-control" *(Galatians 5: 22–23)*. All these characteristics can be found in Jesus, who is a Christian's greatest role model.

LOVE

The most important Christian value is love. Christian love means much more than the kind called "romantic love." In St. Paul's words, "Love is patient and kind; it is not jealous or conceited or proud; love is not ill mannered or selfish or irritable; love does not keep a record of wrongs; love is not happy with evil, but is happy with the truth. Love never gives up; and its faith, hope, and patience will never fail" *(1 Corinthians 13: 4–7)*. This pure love is found in the example of Jesus, who sacrificed everything, including his life, for others. This free gift of love is sometimes called God's grace. It is very important for Christians to show this love not only to fellow Christians, but to everyone, especially the poor and needy, and even to their enemies. Jesus said, "Love your enemies and pray for those who persecute you, so that you may become the sons of your Father in heaven" *(Matthew 5: 44)*.

MOTHER TERESA

Mother Teresa was born in 1910 and died in 1997. She is famous for caring for the poor in Calcutta, India. Many people believe she was a saint and through her work imitated Jesus's love for humanity.

JOY

For Christians, joy is more than just happiness. It is an attitude toward God, the world, and the rest of humanity. Joy is to be found in the company of others and in the glory of God's creation. Joy produces strength of character when a Christian is faced with difficulties. It is a reflection of great faith in God.

SYMBOL OF PEACE
In many services Christians shake hands or embrace each other, saying, "Peace be with you."

PEACE

When Christians go to church they ask God to forgive them for their sins. But before sins can be forgiven, Christians need to forgive each other. Jesus taught that people can have a full relationship with God only when they have a healthy respect for all their neighbors. Therefore, living as a Christian should be about reconciliation—for example, making friends again after a fight or argument. Christians express this idea by sharing the peace; shaking hands or embracing other people in the church. This means that the worshipers have prepared themselves for communion with God in the Eucharist (*see pages 18–19*).

HUMILITY

Humility means not thinking too highly of yourself. By being humble, a Christian does not develop sinful attitudes such as arrogance. Truly humble people are not weak but strong. They are forgiving because they know that nobody, especially themselves, is perfect, and everyone requires the forgiveness of God.

The disciples

The word "disciple" means follower. Some of Jesus's disciples are also called the apostles, meaning missionaries or agents. This indicates that they were chosen to witness the resurrection of Jesus and spread Jesus's teachings after his death. In the Christian tradition the word "disciple" can refer to Jesus's 12 apostles or may be used more widely to describe any Christian. Many Jewish teachers such as Jesus attracted disciples who hoped they would learn from their master and become teachers themselves.

The names of the disciples who were chosen by Jesus to spread his teachings vary in the different Gospels, but St. Mark lists them as:

SIMON (*CALLED PETER BY JESUS*)
JAMES
JOHN
ANDREW
PHILIP
BARTHOLOMEW

MATTHEW
THOMAS
JAMES
THADDAEUS
SIMON THE ZEALOT
JUDAS ISCARIOT (*THE DISCIPLE WHO BETRAYED JESUS TO THE ROMANS*)

WOMEN FOLLOWERS

Several of Jesus's followers were women. This may not seem significant today, but in Jesus's time this would have been very unusual. Women were expected to look after their families at home. Jesus's mother, Mary, and Mary Magdalene were present at the crucifixion. Jesus cured Mary Magdalene of her evil spirits (*Luke 8: 2*) and, according to St. John's Gospel, after his resurrection appeared to her first.

ST. PAUL

St. Paul is sometimes called an apostle because the risen Jesus appeared to him in a vision. He played an important role in the development of Christianity. Paul was a Jew, originally called Saul, who thought the early Christians were taking people away from their Jewish roots and teachings.

Paul was converted to the Christian faith when he saw a vision of Jesus. From that day he became an enthusiastic Christian teacher, and took the name Paul. He went on three missionary journeys and wrote many letters to inspire and encourage the early Christian communities. He founded churches across the Roman Empire.

SAINTS

For all Christians, saints are especially holy people who lived lives devoted to God. Roman Catholics and Orthodox Christians pray to the saints for help and guidance. On November 1, some Christians celebrate All Saints' Day, when they give thanks for the life and works of all the saints. Apart from All Saints' Day, each of the saints has a special day in the year; for example, March 19 is St. Joseph's Day (*see right*). This is called a feast day. In the Roman Catholic Church, feast days are important festivals.

The Bible

The Christians' holy book, the Bible, is made up of the Old Testament and the New Testament. The Bible is a collection of books originally written in the languages of Hebrew and Greek.

A PAGE FROM AN ILLUSTRATED BIBLE

Early Bibles such as this one were hand-written and beautifully decorated.

BOOKS OF THE BIBLE

The Old Testament, which is the Jewish Bible, consists of several books. These include the books of the Law (Genesis to Deuteronomy), the books of History (Joshua to Esther), the books of Wisdom (Job to the Song of Songs) and the books of the Prophets (Isaiah to Malachi).

The New Testament was written after Jesus's death. It consists of the Gospels, the Acts of the Apostles, the Epistles, and a book of visions called the Book of Revelation. Christians use different versions of the Bible. Some contain the Apocrypha (hidden things). These are 14 books of the Old Testament originally composed in Greek, in addition to those written in Hebrew. Protestant Christians do not accept the Apocrypha as having the same importance as the Old and New Testaments and do not usually include them in their versions of the Bible.

THE WORD OF GOD

Some Christians believe the Bible is "the Word of God," and that every word is true because it came directly from God. God made the meaning plain to the people who wrote it down, and therefore, the words of the Bible do not need explaining because their message is timeless.

Other Christians believe the Bible was inspired by God, but that it was written down by people who were limited by the time and place in which they lived. To reveal the truth that all Christians accept it contains, the Bible needs interpreting for the people of today.

PARADING THE BIBLE
As part of this Orthodox service, a highly decorated Bible is carried through a street in Cyprus.

THE USE OF THE BIBLE

Christians use the Bible in a variety of ways. In some churches the Bible is carried as part of a procession. In the Orthodox tradition, the priest carries the Bible into a dimly lit church and, as he appears from behind a screen called the iconostasis, all the lights are turned on. Members of Orthodox churches may also kneel before the Bible or kiss it. In most churches special emphasis is placed on reading the Bible during services. The sermon or talk is often an explanation of a passage from the Bible. People usually stand to show respect when the Gospel is read.

In some Christian countries the Bible has a central role in public life. It is used in political places such as parliaments, or in courts of law when people solemnly promise that they are telling the truth.

The Church

Christians use the word "church" in four ways:

> **1.** The whole, worldwide community of Jesus's followers; also known as "the body of Christ."
>
> **2.** The different denominations, or groups, of the Church that can be found in the world today (*see pages 16–17*).
>
> **3.** Each local community.
>
> **4.** The building that the community uses for worship.

THE BEGINNINGS OF THE CHURCH

Forty days after Jesus's resurrection, he appeared on earth for the last time and ascended to heaven. The Holy Spirit came to his followers 10 days later (50 days after his Resurrection). This event, called Pentecost (*see page 23*), marks the beginning of the Christian Church.

The Church spread to the western part of the Roman Empire, including North Africa. St. Paul (*see page 11*) followed the western trade routes across the Empire to spread the gospel of Christ. The Church also spread east to the Persian Empire and even as far as India: Christian tradition attributes this to St. Thomas.

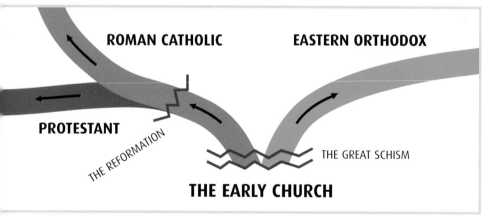

ROMAN CATHOLIC   EASTERN ORTHODOX

PROTESTANT

THE REFORMATION

THE GREAT SCHISM

THE EARLY CHURCH

BRANCHES OF CHRISTIANITY
The diagram above shows how the Christian Church has divided into three main branches since the time of Jesus.

THE GREAT SCHISM

In 1054, growing disagreements between the eastern and western parts of the Church caused them to split. This became known as the Great Schism. The eastern part centered on the city of Constantinople (now Istanbul in Turkey) and was led by the Patriarchs (the bishops of Constantinople, Antioch, Alexandria, and Jerusalem); the western part of the Church was led by the Pope and was centered on Rome.

THE POPE

The Eastern Church did not accept that the Pope had authority over them. They respected him but did not believe he was the most important leader of the Church. The Pope excommunicated the Patriarchs and the members of the Eastern Church, declaring that they were no longer part of God's Church. In response, the Patriarchs excommunicated the Pope.

By the 12th century these differences had resulted in two distinctive forms of Christianity: Eastern Orthodox and Roman Catholic.

THE REFORMATION

The Reformation started in 16th-century Europe as an attempt to reform the Catholic Church. A key figure was Martin Luther (1483–1546), a professor from Germany. He believed the Church should focus on the central Christian message, which is the love of God. Eventually the Church split into Roman Catholicism and Protestantism. Protestant churches became the national churches and rejected the authority of the Pope. In England, King Henry VIII established himself as head of the Church of England (part of the Anglican Church), and today the reigning monarch still holds that position.

POPE JOHN PAUL II
John Paul II became Pope in 1978. The Pope is the head of the Roman Catholic Church. Roman Catholics believe he is the successor of Peter, the leader of the apostles.

THE WORLD COUNCIL OF CHURCHES

Most Christians define their faith in terms of belonging to a particular denomination of the Church. The World Council of Churches, an ecumenical fellowship, was set up in 1948 to help these denominations work together as "the body of Christ." The word "ecumenical" comes from the Greek, *oikoumene,* which means "one world."

SPREAD OF CHRISTIANITY
This map shows the current spread of Christianity and the areas of the world where it is the main religion.

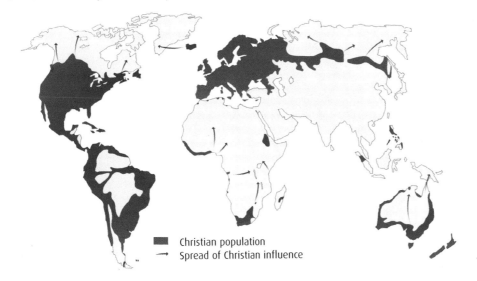

■ Christian population
→ Spread of Christian influence

Different forms of worship

One of the great appeals of Christianity is its diversity. It provides the Gospel message in many different ways to many different cultures. Here are five examples taken from the wide range of Christian groups.

AN ORTHODOX SERVICE
Worshipers stand during the three hours of Divine Liturgy each Sunday.

A QUAKER SERVICE
Members of the Society of Friends sit in silence during morning worship.

THE ORTHODOX CHURCH

Orthodox churches are highly decorated with frescos and icons. These are images of Jesus and the Christian saints, which help the worshipers concentrate. Orthodox churches are usually built in the shape of a cross. The main service, Divine Liturgy, takes place on a Sunday and lasts for about three hours. Services include rituals (actions which carry deeper symbolic meanings): the Bible is carried around the church, and people make the sign of the cross and kiss the icons. The worshipers stand for the whole service.

THE ROMAN CATHOLIC CHURCH

The main act of worship for Roman Catholics is the Mass (*see pages 18–19*). The service lasts for about an hour and includes singing hymns and listening to Bible readings and a sermon. The service is led by a priest, who blesses bread and wine before sharing them with the congregation. The church contains many statues and paintings, especially of the Virgin Mary. Worshipers sit on benches and chairs and face the altar (the table where the priest stands).

THE SOCIETY OF FRIENDS *(Quakers)*

Members of the Society of Friends worship in a Meeting House. This is a plain building containing a room where rows of chairs circle a table, which might hold a focus for worship such as a vase of flowers. During the meeting, which lasts an hour, worshipers sit in silence, waiting for the Holy Spirit to inspire them. People often rise to their feet to speak about something personal, or to comment on a wider issue. People may read something from the Bible or from a Quaker pamphlet called "Notes and Queries." Anyone is allowed to speak at the meeting.

A PENTECOSTAL SERVICE
Pentecostal services are very lively, with joyous singing and clapping in praise of God.

THE CHURCH OF GOD OF PROPHECY

This is one of many black-led, Pentecostal churches found in cities around the world today. Worship concentrates on the preaching of the Word of God—Bible readings and a long sermon. Singing in the church is led by a choir and people playing instruments such as electric guitars and drums. Members clap when singing and give shouts of praise to God such as "Hallelujah" or "Praise to God." People often pray out loud or offer personal accounts about their faith. Services end with a call for people to kneel at a rail at the front of the church and let the Holy Spirit heal any spiritual problems they might have: the pastor, the person leading the service, lays his or her hands on people's heads.

THE ANGLICAN CHURCH

For most Anglicans the main act of worship is the Eucharist, or Holy Communion. It is similar to the Roman Catholic Mass, and is led by a priest or vicar. The service can last for about an hour if it includes hymns. The first part of the service is called the Liturgy of the Word, and the second part is the Liturgy of the Eucharist (*see page 18*). The service includes a sermon, a reading from the Epistles in the New Testament, and a reading from the Old Testament, as well as from one of the Gospels.

PRAYER

Christian worship can also be a private activity involving personal prayer and Bible study. The word "prayer" describes a conversation with God, and it is an important part of a Christian's life. Prayer includes acknowledgment of the glory of God, confession of sins, thanksgiving, explaining of personal needs, and a quiet time for listening to God.

THE LORD'S PRAYER

The most important Christian prayer is the one that Jesus taught to his disciples:
Our Father
Who art in Heaven
Hallowed be thy name
Thy kingdom come
Thy will be done
On earth as it is in heaven.
Give us this day our daily bread
And forgive us our trespasses
As we forgive those who trespass against us.
Lead us not into temptation,
But deliver us from evil.
For thine is the kingdom, the power and the glory,
For ever and ever. Amen.

The last sentence of the Lord's Prayer (*left*) was not included in the original version that appears in the Gospels. It was added at a later date and is not used in some versions of the prayer.

Worship: the Eucharist

The Eucharist (a service in which bread and wine are blessed and eaten) is one of the sacraments—symbols of God's blessing—that help Christians to develop spiritually. For many Christians the Eucharist is the most important of the sacraments. "Eucharist" comes from the Greek word *eucharistia*, meaning "thanksgiving." The name "Eucharist" refers to the thankfulness that Christians feel for what Jesus did for them through his life, death, and resurrection. It also refers to the blessed bread and wine.

A number of other names are also used for this sacrament, such as the Lord's Supper (in memory of Jesus's last meal with his disciples), Mass (the name used by Roman Catholics), and Holy Communion (referring to the closeness to God that occurs during this service).

THE EUCHARIST
Before worshipers receive the bread and wine, it is blessed by the priest or minister.

HOW IS THE EUCHARIST CELEBRATED?

The service is led by a priest or minister. These are men or women who have been trained as Christian leaders. The service may last for about an hour if hymns are sung, but it can last as little as half an hour if the service is just spoken. It is divided into two parts:

1. Liturgy of the Word (the word "liturgy" means divine service): this includes readings from the Bible and sometimes a sermon by the priest or minister.

2. Liturgy of the Eucharist: the priest or minister consecrates some bread and wine. This means that the bread and wine is blessed by the Holy Spirit, who is called down by the priest, and it becomes for the congregation a way of sharing in the death and resurrection of Jesus.

Most Christians use specially made small wafers of bread. Others may use ordinary bread bought from a store. Some serve the wine in a goblet or chalice. In some churches all of the people sharing in the sacrament drink from this cup. Others serve the wine in small individual cups. Methodist Christians use non-alcoholic wine. Some Christian groups celebrate the Eucharist regularly, while others consider it so special that they hold the service less frequently.

WHAT DO THE CONSECRATED BREAD AND WINE MEAN?

The Eucharist is said to be the body and blood of Jesus. Roman Catholic and Orthodox Christians believe that the bread and wine actually become Christ's body and blood at the moment of consecration. Other Christians think of the bread and wine as symbols, and believe that Christ is present in a spiritual way because the bread and wine are reminders of the Last Supper.

WHO CAN TAKE PART?

There are different rules in different churches about who may share in the Eucharist. In some churches all baptized people, however young, may receive the bread and wine; in others only baptized people who have received special preparation and teaching may take part; in yet others only adult members of the church who have confirmed their faith may take part. Finally, in some churches anybody who attends the service may join in.

PREPARING THE BREAD AND WINE
A dish of wafers has been placed on top of a chalice of wine in preparation for the Eucharist.

St. Matthew's Gospel tells how Jesus broke the bread and said, "Take this and eat; this is my body." He then took the cup of wine and said, "Drink from it, all of you. For this is my blood, the blood of the covenant shed for you and for many for the forgiveness of sins." This passage is read every time the Eucharist is celebrated in church.

CELEBRATING HOLY COMMUNION
Christians celebrate the Eucharist to give thanks to Jesus for having died to save them from their sins.

THE CHRISTIAN CALENDAR

Many hundreds of years after Jesus, Christians decided to begin numbering the years again, from the date of his birth. Countries that have been influenced by the Christian religion for a long time divide history into A.D. (Anno Domini, which is Latin for "in the year of the Lord") and B.C. (Before Christ). Today, the terms "Before Common Era" (B.C.E.) and "Common Era" (C.E.) may be used instead of B.C. and A.D.

Not all Christians celebrate their festivals at the same time. For example, Roman Catholic and Anglican Christians follow a different calendar from Orthodox Christians.

ADVENT *(November–December)*

Advent is the start of the Christian year and takes place in the four weeks leading up to Christmas. The word "advent" means "coming." Christians celebrate the coming of Jesus into the world. In churches, the four candles of the advent wreath are lit one by one on each of the four Sundays before Christmas. This shows that Jesus is the light of the world.

Today, many churches hold a Christingle service at the end of Advent. A Christingle is an orange with a candle inserted in the top. A red ribbon is fastened around the middle of the orange and four toothpicks containing fruit and nuts are inserted into it.

THE CHRISTINGLE SERVICE

The orange of the Christingle represents the world; the candle represents Jesus who brought light to the world. The red ribbon reminds Christians of the death of Jesus, and the four toothpicks represent the four seasons and the fruits of the Earth given by God.

CHRISTMAS *(December 25/ January 6 or 7)*

Christmas celebrates the birth of Jesus on December 25, with the exception of the Eastern Orthodox Church, which celebrates it on January 7. Christmas is celebrated all over the world, and people attend church services, give presents to one another in the way the wise men gave presents to Jesus, decorate their homes, send greeting cards to each other, and celebrate with feasting and parties. Christmas is also a time for visiting friends and relatives.

EPIPHANY
In many countries in Europe, such as Austria (*above*), and in South America, Epiphany is celebrated with a parade.

EPIPHANY *(January 6)*

In western churches, Epiphany celebrates the time Jesus was brought gifts of gold, frankincense, and myrrh by the wise men. He was revealed to them, and to all people, as the Son of God. In eastern churches, Epiphany celebrates the baptism of Jesus. Epiphany also marks the end of the 12 Days of Christmas, the final day of Christmas celebrations.

SHROVE TUESDAY *(February/March)*

This is the day before the start of Lent *(see below)*. The name comes from the word "shriven," which means to confess your sins and be forgiven. Shrove Tuesday is also called Pancake Day and Mardi Gras (Fat Tuesday).

ASH WEDNESDAY *(February/March)*

This is the first day of Lent *(see below)*, 40 days before Easter Sunday. In some churches the priest makes a mark of the cross in ash on the forehead of worshipers. It is a sign of mortality (the fact that people eventually die) and penitence (saying sorry for doing wrong).

LENT *(February-March/April)*

This is the period leading up to Easter. Traditionally, Lent is a time for people to fast (give up certain foods) and think seriously, and symbolizes Christians sharing in the 40 days that Jesus spent in the desert.

PALM SUNDAY *(March/April)*

Palm Sunday is the beginning of Holy Week, the last week in the life of Jesus. On Palm Sunday, as Jesus rode into Jerusalem on a donkey, the crowds shouted, "Blessings on him who comes in the name of the Lord!" At the same time, they laid palm leaves on the road in front of him. Today, many Christians celebrate Palm Sunday with the Eucharist, during which everyone is given a cross made from a palm leaf.

THE LAST SUPPER BY LEONARDO DA VINCI

Christians celebrate Jesus's last meal with his disciples on Holy Thursday. The Last Supper is remembered by them in the celebration of the Eucharist.

HOLY THURSDAY or MAUNDY THURSDAY *(March/April)*

This is the Thursday before Easter, and it commemorates the last meal that Jesus and his disciples had together. During the supper, which Christians now call the Last Supper, Jesus washed his disciples' feet. This was a sign that after Jesus's death, the disciples should go out and serve other people. It was also an act of humility, which is an important Christian value *(see pages 8–9)*.

GOOD FRIDAY *(March/April)*

Good Friday is a very solemn day on which Christians remember the day Jesus was crucified. It is called Good Friday because Christians believe that this is the day when good conquered evil. In churches everything is very bare, with no flowers or decorations.

EASTER *(March/April)*

Easter is the most important Christian festival, symbolizing three momentous Christian beliefs: that God is love, that Jesus is the savior of the world, and that Jesus is alive today. The Gospels tell how three days after Jesus's death, some of his followers went to the tomb where his body had been laid, only to find it empty. Later, Jesus appeared to them to confirm that he had risen from the dead. In most Roman Catholic and Anglican churches there is a special service either on Saturday night or very early on Sunday morning.

EASTER SERVICE
People come together at Easter to praise Jesus.

A Paschal (Easter) Candle is lit, sometimes from a bonfire outside the church. The priest carries the candle into the church, and worshipers use it to light their own small candles. The darkness of the church is lit up by the candles to symbolize the resurrection of Jesus.

Easter Sunday celebrates the resurrection of Jesus from the dead. Services are joyful occasions when people shout, "Christ is risen. He is risen indeed. Hallelujah." Many churches are decorated with fresh spring flowers.

ASCENSION DAY *(May/June)*

This celebrates the 40th day after Easter Sunday and marks the last appearance of Jesus on Earth. It is always celebrated on a Thursday.

PENTECOST *(May/June)*

Pentecost (from a Greek word meaning "50") is held 50 days after Easter Sunday and is the celebration of the birthday of the Christian Church. Christians praise the coming of the Holy Spirit to the followers of Jesus 50 days after his resurrection, and the formation of the first community of believers (the Church). By the power of the Holy Spirit, the Christian Church carries on the work begun by Jesus.

HARVEST FESTIVAL *(September/October)*

This festival was first established in Europe in the 14th century. Christians come together to celebrate God as Creator and thank him for the Earth's rich resources. Churches are decorated with arrangements of food, which are later distributed to poor and elderly people.

Jesus was crucified in Jerusalem before the Jewish Passover festival. Several hundred years later, many Christians felt that their festival of Easter should not get confused with the Jewish festival. Sunday was the Christians' holy day, because it was on a Sunday that Jesus rose from the dead. They decided that Easter should be celebrated on the Sunday following the first full moon after the vernal equinox (the day in spring when day and night are the same length). As a result Easter is held on a different date every year.

Sacred places

It is not a duty for Christians to go on pilgrimages (religious journeys). However, Christians have been making pilgrimages for hundreds of years, and they were especially common during the Middle Ages (c. A.D. 1000–1453). Because Christianity is a worldwide religion, there are many places of great significance to followers.

MEDIEVAL PILGRIMS
People began to visit the Holy Land following the defeat of the Turks during the First Crusade (1096–99).

THE HOLY LAND

Many Christians visit the places where Jesus lived and taught. These include Bethlehem, Nazareth, and Jerusalem. The Church of the Nativity, where many Christians believe Jesus was born, is in Bethlehem. Inside the church are a number of altars, including those of the Orthodox, Roman Catholic, and Coptic (Egyptian) Churches. In Nazareth, where Jesus grew up, are the sites of the Basilica of the Annunciation and the Greek Orthodox Church of St. Gabriel. Both claim to be the place where the Angel Gabriel announced to Mary that she was to give birth to Jesus. In Jerusalem the Church of the Holy Sepulchre is thought to cover the places where Jesus was crucified and buried. Inside the church there is a block of stone, on which many believe the body of Jesus rested after he died. There are a number of altars inside this church, representing Greek Orthodox, Roman Catholic, and the Armenian, Syrian, Coptic, and Ethiopian Churches.

ROME

Roman Catholics, in particular, visit Rome to see the Vatican City. This is a tiny independent state within Rome itself that contains the famous church called St. Peter's. Christian tradition says that St. Peter is buried beneath the church. It is also believed that St. Paul was martyred in Rome. A monastery was founded in the seventh century on the spot where he was believed to have died. Christians also visit Rome because the Vatican is the home of the Pope, the head of the Roman Catholic Church.

LOURDES

Lourdes is in southern France and is a popular place of pilgrimage. It was in Lourdes that St. Bernadette, a sickly child, had a vision of the Virgin Mary in 1858. At the spot where Bernadette had the vision a spring of water appeared, and it is said to have healing powers. Since that time, many sick people have visited Lourdes in the hope of a cure. Some report that they have indeed been cured by the holy water.

TAIZÉ

Taizé is a modern place of pilgrimage, especially popular with young people. It lies in southeast France and was founded by a protestant, Brother Roger Schutz, after World War II. Brother Roger wanted to establish a center of pilgrimage where young people of any religion, or no religion at all, could visit to talk and worship. Visitors often camp in the fields and do chores around the site. Taizé worship consists of beautiful, simple songs, often sung in Latin.

PILGRIMS AT LOURDES

Lourdes is visited by thousands of Christians each year.

25

Life rituals

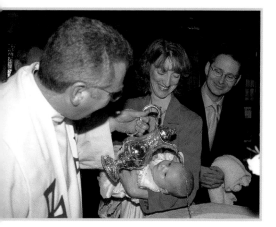

BAPTIZING A BABY
Many Christians baptize their babies. The water symbolizes the washing away of sin.

Like anyone else, Christians celebrate important times of their lives. Celebrations of birth, growing up, marriage, and death are all connected to Christian sacraments (symbols of God's blessing).

BAPTISM OR CHRISTENING

At this ceremony, a baby joins the Church and is given his or her Christian names. Adults can also be baptized. It is an important step towards salvation and marks a commitment to turn away from the power of sin and towards God. When a baby is baptized, a number of people are invited to be godparents. They promise to look after the spiritual well-being of the child. The priest or minister pours holy water on the person's head. In some churches, particularly when adults are baptized, the person's whole body is immersed in water. The water symbolizes that the person's sin is washed away. This goes back to the time when people, including Jesus, were baptized in the river Jordan. The word itself comes from the Greek word *baptizo*, which means "to dip."

SYMBOLS OF BAPTISM

Apart from the water, there are other symbols involved in baptism. The priest or minister may make a sign of the cross on the person's forehead. The person being baptized may wear white clothes, symbolizing purity. The parents of most baptized children, or baptized adults, are given a lighted candle, symbolizing Jesus, the light of the world.

CONFIRMATION

In the Christian Church, people are usually confirmed in their early teens. Confirmation means that they have accepted Christianity for themselves. Before confirmation, there is a period of religious study and possibly a time of silence and solitude. At the confirmation ceremony, the bishop (a leader among the priests, with the spiritual authority to confirm) places his hands on their head and prays that the Holy Spirit may come to them and guide them. After this the person can take part in Holy Communion. In the Roman

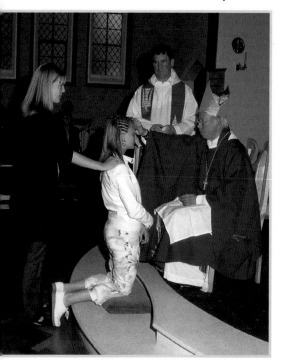

A CONFIRMATION
A bishop calls on the Holy Spirit to act as a guide.

Catholic Church, children have their First Communion at about age seven, before they are confirmed in their early teens. In the Orthodox Church, children are often baptized and confirmed as babies at the same time in a ceremony called *chrismation*.

MARRIAGE

A traditional Christian marriage takes place in a church, with the blessing of God. During the service, the bride and groom make solemn vows in front of God to love one another and stay faithful to each other forever. "Man must not separate, then, what God has joined together" (*Matthew 19: 6*).

DEATH

When a Christian is dying, fellow Christians often visit, and they may read the Bible and pray together. A priest or minister may celebrate Holy Communion with the dying person and anoint him or her with oil. The dying person may also make a confession of sins to God. Shortly after the person has died, there is a funeral service. This includes Bible readings, hymns, and prayers expressing the Christian belief that after death a person has new life with God.

A MARRIAGE SERVICE

Marriage is a sacrament for some Christians. This couple is exchanging rings as a sign of their commitment to each other.

BURIAL

Traditionally, Christians are buried in churchyards. Today, many people choose to be cremated. Their bodies are burnt to ashes: "Ashes to ashes, dust to dust." The Christian view is that it does not really matter what happens to the body once the soul has departed; the soul will have gone to heaven, to be with God.

HEAVEN AND HELL

Historically, heaven and hell have been imagined as physical places where souls go after death, and some very extreme images of hell, in particular, were developed in the Middle Ages. These images are not really in keeping with most modern Christian ideas. For Christians, heaven is being with God, and hell is being apart from God.

Christian denominations

ROMAN CATHOLIC CHURCH

NUMBER OF WORSHIPERS	DATE FOUNDED	WHERE PRACTICED	PLACE OF WORSHIP	LEADER OF WORSHIP	MAIN FEATURES
900 million worldwide	Roman Catholics date the founding of their Church back to the early Christian community. St. Peter is claimed to have been the first Bishop of Rome. The Roman Church split from the Eastern Church in 1054.	worldwide	church	priest, bishop	• The Pope is the head of the Church. • Tradition, as well as holy scripture, is an important source of faith and practice. • The Church recognizes seven sacraments: baptism, confirmation, the Eucharist, penance, extreme unction, ordination, marriage. • Mass is the most important act of worship. • The Virgin Mary is very important to Catholics, as she was the mother of Jesus. • Confession: for Roman Catholics, it is important that they regularly confess their sins to a priest.

ORTHODOX CHURCHES

THE ORIENTAL ORTHODOX CHURCH

NUMBER OF WORSHIPERS	DATE FOUNDED	WHERE PRACTICED	PLACE OF WORSHIP	LEADER OF WORSHIP	MAIN FEATURES
30 million	The Eastern Church traces its origins back to the early Christian community. In A.D. 451, some Eastern bishops formed the Eastern Oriental Church.	Armenian Church, Coptic Church (Egypt), Ethiopian Orthodox Church, Syrian Jacobite Church	church	priest, bishop	• Orthodox Churches place great importance on tradition, as well as holy scripture. • The most important act of worship is Divine Liturgy. • The Church recognizes the same seven sacraments as the Roman Catholic Church. • Orthodox Christianity stresses mystery and worship involving all the senses. • Icons (sacred pictures) play an important part in Orthodox worship.

THE EASTERN ORTHODOX CHURCH

NUMBER OF WORSHIPERS	DATE FOUNDED	WHERE PRACTICED	PLACE OF WORSHIP	LEADER OF WORSHIP	MAIN FEATURES
120 million	1054, when the Eastern and Western Churches finally split.	Eastern Orthodox Churches of Greece, Russia, Bulgaria, Cyprus, Serbia, Georgia, Romania, Poland, Albania, Czechoslovakia	church	priest, bishop	• Like Roman Catholics, the Orthodox Churches place great importance on tradition, as well as holy scripture. • The most important act of worship is Divine Liturgy. • The Church recognizes the same seven sacraments as the Roman Catholic Church. • Orthodox Christianity stresses mystery and worship involving all the senses. • Icons (sacred pictures) play an important part in Orthodox worship.

ANGLICAN CHURCHES

THE CHURCH OF ENGLAND

NUMBER OF WORSHIPERS	DATE FOUNDED	WHERE PRACTICED	PLACE OF WORSHIP	LEADER OF WORSHIP	MAIN FEATURES
1–2 million. There are approximately 70 million Anglicans worldwide.	In 1534, the monarch of England became the supreme head of the Church after Parliament passed the Act of Supremacy, which renounced the authority of the Pope. In 1571, 39 articles defined the doctrine and ritual of the Church.	England	church	bishop, vicar, rector, curate	• The Church of England is an "established Church." This means the King or Queen of the country is the head of the Church. Church of England bishops can sit in Parliament. • As a result of the Reformation in Europe, the scriptures are all that is needed for salvation. • Only two sacraments are celebrated: Holy Communion (the Eucharist) and baptism. • Worship: some is very like Roman Catholic worship (called "High Church"). Other worship is less formal, such as the Free Church or Evangelical worship. This is sometimes called "Low Church." • The Anglican Church now ordains women to be priests.

THE EPISCOPAL CHURCH

NUMBER OF WORSHIPERS	DATE FOUNDED	WHERE PRACTICED	PLACE OF WORSHIP	LEADER OF WORSHIP	MAIN FEATURES
2.75 million	Founded in 1784 by Anglican settlers. Samuel Seabury was the first Bishop of Connecticut. The name "The Episcopal Church" was accepted in 1967.	Scotland and the U.S.	church	bishop, vicar, rector, curate	• The scriptures are all that is needed for salvation. • Only two sacraments are celebrated: Holy Communion (the Eucharist) and baptism. • Worship: see entry for the Church of England. • The Anglican Church now ordains women to be priests.

NB. Many countries have their own branch of the Anglican Church. In Scotland it is called the Episcopal Church; in Wales, the Church in Wales. There are Anglican Churches all over the world, including the Anglican Churches of Australia and Canada.

OTHER PROTESTANT CHURCHES

THE LUTHERAN CHURCH

NUMBER OF WORSHIPERS	DATE FOUNDED	WHERE PRACTICED	PLACE OF WORSHIP	LEADER OF WORSHIP	MAIN FEATURES
60 million	1530. Named after Martin Luther, who is regarded as the founder of the Protestant Reformation. His main belief was that faith alone was necessary for salvation.	It is the state church in most Scandinavian countries, but it is active throughout the world.	church	pastor	• The Bible is the sole source of faith. • Hymns are an important part of worship, and services include a sermon based on the Bible. • The Book of Covenant, published in 1577, contains the beliefs of the Lutherans. • Most Lutheran churches belong to the Lutheran World Federation, whose headquarters are in Geneva, Switzerland.

METHODISTS

NUMBER OF WORSHIPERS	DATE FOUNDED	WHERE PRACTICED	PLACE OF WORSHIP	LEADER OF WORSHIP	MAIN FEATURES
26 million	1739, by John Wesley. Wesley was a major figure in the Evangelical Revival in the 18th century. He rejected some of the teachings and practices of the Church of England, and Methodists became a separate group in 1795.	worldwide but especially in the UK and the U.S.	church, chapel	minister	• Methodists live in accordance with the teachings of the Bible. • Emphasis is placed on the Holy Spirit and a close personal relationship with God. • Worship is simple, and there is emphasis on a partnership between ministers and the ordinary worshipers (laity). • Methodists do not drink alcohol, so wine is not used in the Eucharist.

REFORMED CHURCHES (Presbyterians)

NUMBER OF WORSHIPERS	DATE FOUNDED	WHERE PRACTICED	PLACE OF WORSHIP	LEADER OF WORSHIP	MAIN FEATURES
40 million	1535. John Calvin, like Luther, had reformist views. He traveled to Geneva, where he founded the reformed church.	Worldwide. Because Calvin preached that Christian principles should influence the state, Presbyterians often got involved in politics. This led to the founding of national Presbyterian Churches, such as the Scottish Presbyterian Church, founded in 1560 by John Knox; it is the state church of Scotland.	church	minister	• The Bible is all that is needed for faith. • Belief in predestination: the idea that God decides who is to be saved and who should be damned, and that the individual cannot resist God's will. • Belief that the state should conform to the will of God, leading to political involvement by Presbyterian Christians.

THE SALVATION ARMY

NUMBER OF WORSHIPERS	DATE FOUNDED	WHERE PRACTICED	PLACE OF WORSHIP	LEADER OF WORSHIP	MAIN FEATURES
4 million	In 1865, by William Booth, a Methodist minister, in London. At that time it was called the Christian Mission. It became known as the Salvation Army in 1878.	worldwide in over 70 countries	citadel	The movement became organized along army lines, with a uniform and members being given the same titles as soldiers. The head of the Salvation Army is called a general.	• Conducts open-air meetings involving brass bands. • Runs hostels for the homeless, rehabilitation centers for alcoholics, hospitals, food kitchens. • Believe that the Bible is divinely inspired, and preaching is the central part of services, but music is very important. • Women are seen as equal to men in all spheres.

MORE PROTESTANT CHURCHES

BAPTISTS

NUMBER OF WORSHIPERS	DATE FOUNDED	WHERE PRACTICED	PLACE OF WORSHIP	LEADER OF WORSHIP	MAIN FEATURES
There are approximately 100 million Baptists worldwide.	1611. Thomas Helwys founded a church in Spitalfields, London, that emphasized believers' baptism rather than infant baptism. This eventually led to the formation of the Baptist Missionary Society in 1792.	Worldwide. In 1639 the Church spread from the UK to the U.S. where it is a strong and varied Church.	church	minister	• Only those who are old enough and able to profess a personal faith in Christ should be baptized. • It emphasizes missionary work because even Christians can fall from grace and so need to be taught the gospel. • Worship strongly emphasizes the Bible and preaching.

SOCIETY OF FRIENDS (Quakers)

NUMBER OF WORSHIPERS	DATE FOUNDED	WHERE PRACTICED	PLACE OF WORSHIP	LEADER OF WORSHIP	MAIN FEATURES
280,000	1650, by George Fox. The name Quaker probably refers to the statement from George Fox that people should "quake at the word of the Lord."	Worldwide but particularly in the UK and U.S. to which William Penn, escaping persecution, fled in 1682. He established the first Quaker colony in Pennsylvania.	meeting house	One of the main principles of the Friends is that there is no need for a ministry. Therefore, meetings are not actually led by anyone, although senior Quakers called "elders" do oversee them.	• The rejection of a ministry. • Quakers do not celebrate the traditional Christian sacraments, believing all life is sacred (holy) and no place is more sacred than any other. • God is often referred to as the inner light which is present in everyone. • Worship is largely silent, punctuated only when a Friend is moved by the inner light, or the Holy Spirit, to say something. • Quakers have always placed great emphasis on social work.

PENTECOSTAL (Charismatic)

NUMBER OF WORSHIPERS	DATE FOUNDED	WHERE PRACTICED	PLACE OF WORSHIP	LEADER OF WORSHIP	MAIN FEATURES
250 million (although there are many charismatic Christians in other denominations).	The beginning of the 20th century, in the U.S. It became organized in Los Angeles in 1905. The movement reached Britain in 1907. In the 1960s, Christians in other denominations claimed that they had received the "gifts of the Spirit." This was the beginning of the Charismatic Movement within the Church as a whole. The word comes from "charism," which means gift. This movement is the fastest growing in the Christian Church today.	There are many Pentecostal denominations, especially in the U.S. and the UK. These include many black-led churches; for example, the Church of God of Prophecy and the New Testament Church of God. More recently, the House Church movement has grown rapidly.	church	pastor	• Emphasizes the "gifts of the Spirit" received by the apostles at the first Pentecost. • Worship is informal and emphasizes the literal interpretation of the Bible in preaching, enthusiastic singing, and spontaneous exclamations of praise. • Emphasizes healing by the Holy Spirit. Worship often ends with the pastor and other members laying their hands on people in the congregation.

EVANGELICALS

Evangelicals are Christians of any denomination, and evangelicalism has been present in the Church since the early Christians. It is a movement that grew rapidly in the latter half of the 20th century—today one in four Christians worldwide claims to be evangelical. The Evangelical Alliance was founded in 1846, and represents evangelical Christians and their churches on an international basis. Today there are many churches that call themselves evangelical. Many are small, local churches, often meeting in school halls or other public buildings.

MAIN FEATURES

• Belief in the Bible as the literal word of God. It contains no errors because the Holy Spirit inspired all the writers. So what was true when the Bible was written is also true today.
• Belief that the Bible is the center of a Christian life, and so Bible study is very important.
• Emphasize conversion or being born again, leaving behind a life of sin and beginning a new life centered on Christ as personal Savior.

Glossary

ADAM AND EVE The first man and woman created by God.

APOSTLE One of the 12 disciples chosen by Jesus to go out into the world and spread the gospel.

BIBLE The Christians' holy book, made up of the Old Testament and the New Testament.

BISHOP A leader of all the churches in a particular area. A bishop has the power to ordain priests and perform confirmation.

COMMANDMENT A command from God.

CONSECRATION The blessing of the bread and wine for the Eucharist.

CRUCIFIXION An extremely long and painful way of killing someone by nailing their hands and feet to a cross.

DENOMINATION A group which accepts the same rules and believes in the same thing. Two Christian denominations are Anglicans and Roman Catholics.

DISCIPLE A person who accepts the teachings of a leader and passes on what they have learned to other people. Jesus had 12 disciples.

EUCHARIST A sacrament, also called the Lord's Supper, Mass, and Holy Communion, in which bread and wine are blessed and eaten. "Eucharist" also refers to the blessed bread and wine.

EXCOMMUNICATE To exclude a member of the Church from taking part in its activities and communal prayers.

GETHSEMANE The garden in Jerusalem where Jesus was betrayed by Judas.

GOSPELS The first four books of the Bible, which contain the story of Jesus's life and teachings. They were written by Mark, Matthew, Luke, and John.

THE HOLY SPIRIT The third part of the Holy Trinity.

THE HOLY TRINITY The union of the three different aspects of God: God the Father, God the Son, and God the Holy Spirit.

INCARNATE Something which takes on a bodily form, especially a human one. Jesus was God incarnate.

THE LAST SUPPER The last meal Jesus had with his disciples, at which he told them he would be killed.

MARTYR A person who is killed for refusing to give up their religious beliefs.

THE NICENE CREED A statement of belief written down by early Christians.

PATRIARCHS The leading bishops of the early Christian community and the leading bishops of the Orthodox Church today.

POPE The leader of the Roman Catholic Church and the successor of Peter.

THE REFORMATION An attempt to reform the Catholic Church, begun in the 16th century.

RESURRECTION Jesus's return to life three days after his crucifixion.

SACRAMENTS These are symbols of God's blessing that help Christians to develop spirituality. They are: baptism, penance, confirmation, the Eucharist (the Lord's Supper, Mass, or Holy Communion), holy orders, marriage, and blessing the sick and dying.

SALVATION Being saved from the power of sin.

SCRIPTURES The sacred writings of a religion.

SIN An act or thought which goes against God's rules.

SOUL The spirit of a person that exists separately from the body. Christians believe that after death, the soul of a person goes to heaven (to be with God), or to hell (to be apart from God).

VIRGIN Someone who has never had sexual intercourse.

ZEALOT A member of the extreme Jewish political party that resisted Roman rule during the first century A.D.

Index